this notebook
belongs
to

Table of Contents

No.	Topic	Page

Table of Contents

Table of Contents

Date:

4

Date:

6

Date:

Date:

14

Date:

Date:

Date:

20

Date:

Date:

28

Date:

Date:

Date:

Date:

Date:

Date:

Date:

Date:

Date:

Date:

Date:

Date:

Date:

Date:

Date:

Date:

Date:

Date:

Date:

Date:

Date:

Date:

Date:

Date:

Date:

Date:

Date:

Date:

Important Contacts:

Important Contacts:

Made in the USA
Monee, IL
04 October 2022

15207157R00063